MW01198905

Sleaze & Slander

SLEAZE & SLANDER

New and Selected Comic Verse, 1995–2015

Poems by

A.M. Juster

Measure Press
Evansville, Indiana

The text of this book is composed in Baskerville.
Composition by R.G.
Manufacturing by Ingram.

Juster, A.M.
  Sleaze & Slander: New and Selected Comic Verse, 1995–2015 / by A.M. Juster
— 1st ed.

  ISBN-13: 978-1-939574-14-5
  ISBN-10: 1-939574-14-5
  Library of Congress Control Number: 2016903975

Measure Press
526 S. Lincoln Park Dr.
Evansville, IN 47714
http://www.measurepress.com/measure/

Acknowledgments

The author wishes to thank the editors of the publications in which these poems have appeared, sometimes in a slightly different form.

Able Muse: Martial 10.47, 12.61
Angle: "Poem of the Prick"
Arion: "Epitaph for a Drunken Twit"
Asses of Parnassus: "Epitaph for a Star of Reality Shows" and Martial 1.83
Barefoot Muse: "Houseguests"
The Classical Outlook: Martial 1.4, 1.28, 3.18, 3.54, 4.38, 7.65, 8.35, 8.69, 9.9, 10.43, "Selected Problems in Interspecies Relationships As Exemplified in Classical Mythology"
Edge City Review: Martial 1.23, 1.73, "On the Death of B.F. Skinner"
Evansville Review: "Love Song," "Poem of the Pussy"
First Things: "A Stern Warning to Canada," "Disclaimer," "Elegy for a Horseshoe Crab," "Rejection Note for *Paradise Regained*," "Revisionism," "Self-portrait at Fifty"
The Formalist: "Botches," "Letter to Auden," Martial 8.43, "Philomusus the Grammarian," "To a Statue of Rufus the Rhetorician"
Hellas: "Myron Begged Lisa for Sex"
Hipster Conservative: "The Supreme Court Drinking Song"
Light: "A Consolation of Aging," "After 277 Years, Another Birthday Poem for Esther Johnson, a Long-term 'Houseguest' of the Reverend Jonathan Swift," "Backup Plan," "For Jim Henson," "Gift Shop Blues," "Grandmother Gives Birth to Chimp," "Greeting Card Verse for Unusual Occasions," "Juice," "Long Strange Trip," "Honest Email to the Librarian of Congress," Martial 4.48, 7.3, 12.69, "Mismatch," "Mistakes Were Made"
Los Angeles Times: "A Prayer to Bill Gates"
Measure: "Modern Lullaby"
The Paris Review: "Visions of the Serengeti"
Per Contra: "Advice for My Comrades," "Prufrock's Thirteen Ways of Looking at a Red Wheelbarrow Glazed with Rain beside White Chickens"
Post Road: "A Plea to My Vegan Great-Grandchildren"
The Weekly Standard: "A Panegyric for Presidents' Day"

"Poem of the Pussy" was a co-winner of 2015 Willis Barnstone Translation Prize.

The Horace translations appeared in *The Satires of Horace* (University of Pennsylvania Press, 2008).

The five Billy Collins poems will appear in *The Billy Collins Experience* (White Violet Press, 2016)

I want to thank my editors at *Light*, Melissa Balmain and the late John Mella, for their inexplicable support. I also want to thank Aaron Poochigian for his sound advice on many of my Latin translations.

"We are all in the gutter, but some of us are looking at the stars."
— *Oscar Wilde,* Lady Windermere's Fan

CONTENTS

I. Outside Jokes

II. Inside Jokes

III. The Stuttering Ventriloquist

IV. Shrapnel

I. Outside Jokes

Grandmother Gives Birth to Chimp

You never know what ends up being true.
Amelia Earhart flew to Timbuktu,
then on to Kansas to escape it all.
The Loch Ness Monster is quite real, though small,
and lonely OJ never had a clue.

Experts say Elvis only had the flu,
Houdini's ghost is merely overdue,
And someday Roswell's aliens may call.
You never know.

Though true believers dwindle to a few,
don't doubt the CIA has lied to you.
Don't cringe when cynics call us "off the wall"!
Thank God the tabloids keep us on the ball!
Stay tuned — no matter what you thought you knew,
you never know.

Backup Plan

If I were single once again
(not that I'm really planning, dear),
I would indulge! Like other men,

I'd bag the low-fat regimen
and live on burgers, ribs and beer.
If I were single, once again

there would be Fritos in the den,
and napkin rings would disappear.
I would indulge like other men,

not shave or floss, and sleep past ten.
My feelings could be insincere.
If I were single once again,

and free to leave the seat up when
my heart desired, it is clear
I would indulge like other men —

although I *would* be helpless then,
and yearn for your return. I fear,
if I were single once again,
I would indulge like other men.

Proposed Clichés

Softer than an old potato
too moldy to mash.

More user-friendly than a hooker
hard up for cash.

Love is like a hard-time sentence —
but better than cancer.

Ask not what your country can do,
for fear of the answer.

Beauty beheld is merely skin-deep;
infections are deeper.

The price of honesty can be steep;
candidates are cheaper.

A drowning man may clutch at straws,
but his sipping is pathetic.

Burn the candle at both ends
if you want to wax poetic.

You can call off your dogs,
but your cats will ignore you.

If actuaries had wings,
they still would just bore you.

An apple a day keeps the doctor away,
but not your disease.

Blood is thicker than water
except when they freeze.

It's all spilt milk under the bridge,
so don't be big babies.

If you're crazy like a fox,
get tested for rabies.

Visions of the Serengeti

When Mutual of Omaha supported
nature shows, it spared us sex and gore.
We stared as peacocks preened and rhinos courted,
then later saw the litters — nothing more.
The mother wombats would protect their young
(just as insurance agents do for you)
and Marlon would relax while Jim's life hung
in balance, for their dart gun's aim was true.

I watch new nature shows now with my spaniel.
She wags her tail as jackals disembowel
the wildebeest of The Discovery Channel,
then warns off flapping vultures with a growl.
Her rapture grows until the carnage stops,
then she considers me and licks her chops.

Long Strange Trip

The flower children gone to seed
Bake brownies for the PTA
And give to liberals in need.

Their ponytails display some gray
And nothing tie-dyed ever fits
Despite the tofu and sorbet.

Now they are mocked as "hippie-crits"
By free-range children who refuse
To heed their parents' tired views
On love and peace and endless summer.

What a bummer.

The Supreme Court Drinking Song

Let's buy another round! Let's buy another round!
We'll pass no bar in town until our fears are drowned!
Show Congress we are wild!
Ignore appeals they filed!
Who cares what precedents they found?
Let's buy another round!
We'll pass no bar in town until our fears are drowned!

O bailiff, bring more beer! O bailiff, bring more beer!
Our First Amendment rights have never been more clear!
Forget what lawyers cite —
Let's drop our briefs tonight!
There are no cases we must hear,
So bailiff, bring more beer!
Our First Amendment rights have never been more clear!

These robes keep getting hot! These robes keep getting hot!
Our livers may be shot, but we've got guts to rot!
O citizens united,
Let's toast the unindicted!
A brew or two would help a lot;
These robes keep getting hot!
Our livers may be shot, but we've got guts to rot!

We're final in the end! We're final in the end!
No more appeals no matter what your lawyers spend!
It's time to test our mettle —
Tell parties they must settle!
There's nothing shysters can defend;
We're final in the end!
No more appeals no matter what your lawyers spend!

We'll end the 5-4's! We'll end the 5-4's!
Let's drink, opine and puke until they close the doors!
When things start getting tense,
We'll write no more dissents!
So screw the *Bushes versus Gores*,
We'll end the 5-4's!
Let's drink, opine and puke until they close the doors!

A Prayer to Bill Gates

O ye who giveth Word to every town,
Who doth decide when Windows shutteth down,
Who taught thy servants how to interface
And lordeth over stars of Cyberspace:
We call to Thee, though Thou shalt not reply;
Let us not be the Apple of thine eye.
Smite all Nigerians with propositions,
The heretics' unauthorized editions,
The bugs and viruses that blight our land,
Commands that only prophets understand,
And Vista's demon spawn! Lord, hear our cries!
May e-mail not lament our penis size,
May all thine FAQ's be clearly written,
And plagues of evil regulators smitten!
Show mercy for the lost of AOL —
Deliver them from their Time Warner Hell.
Bless sweet Melinda, mother of thine heirs!
O scourge of Satan's programs, hear our prayers!

Modern Lullaby

Sleep, little baby, and don't you cry;
Momma's singin' you a lullaby.
"Daddy" doesn't care where we have been;
You don't see no cigarettes and gin.

Sleep, restless baby, and then be still;
I don't think you want more Benadryl.
Dream sweet dreams about your teddy bears,
Not that guy who's comin' up the stairs.

Rest little darlin', and don't you sob;
Momma's got some buddies in The Mob.
Don't go squealin' this to anyone:
Santa's makin' you a big-boy gun.

Cops may stop just to say hello;
"Daddy" doesn't really need to know.
Momma's gonna have her alibi;
So dream, weary child, and don't you cry.

A Plea to My Vegan Great-Grandchildren

It is my hope you will agree
I lack responsibility
for disco, Vista and *The View*;
consider me a victim too.
I wasn't all that keen on war
or most oppression of the poor,
and please believe that I regret
your payments on our Chinese debt.
Oh sure, I looked the other way
from toxic waste and Tom Delay,
but I still paid most bills on time
and uncut nose hair's not a crime.
I never took to gangsta rap
or built a mindless killer app.
I'm sure you cringe at meat I ate,
but bacon always tasted great
and barbecue, when smoked just right,
was such a sensual delight
. . . though now I'm being more objective
and see it from the pig's perspective.
Despite these sordid legacies,
can't you condone some eggs and cheese?
Perhaps for some unique occasion?
You may require more persuasion,
so I will make my best defense:
for all my sins, I had the sense

to marry someone, I would guess,
who lessened your genetic mess
and made you brilliant, strong and kind —
and sensitive where I was blind —
so muster Wiccan charity
and please do not disparage me.

Mistakes Were Made

Your check was probably mislaid;
I guarantee you will be paid.

My people screwed up on their own;
I would have stopped them had I known.

The problem must be what I feared:
the Internet is acting weird.

I never thought it was a crime;
everyone does it all the time.

I didn't know there was a cop;
I must have been too drunk to stop.

My mother was a piece of work;
she didn't mean to raise a jerk.

A Panegyric
for Presidents' Day

In malls today it is inhuman
Not to talk of Taft or Truman,
Nor should a shopper crack a joke
Evoking faults of Ford and Polk.
Make Roosevelts a Facebook "like"
And generally embrace our Ike.
No matter what you may have heard,
Toast Silent Cal — without a word.
May Andrew Johnson now receive
Our pity and a brief reprieve.
Until tomorrow pardon Nixon
As well as every Clinton vixen.
Let food courts ring with Taylor's praise!
Remember Rutherford B. Hayes,
Those Millard Fillmore glory days,
Ulysses S. — plus his white horse —
Van Buren, Tyler too, of course,
And celebrate, this chilly day,
Young JFK and LBJ.
Let rancor fade and no one mock
Buchanan, Bushes or Barack.
Thank Washington and James Monroe —
And everybody, friend or foe,
Republican or Democrat:
Don't mix up Garfield with that cat!
Avoid unfair comparisons
When speaking of the Harrisons.

Tom Jefferson and Franklin Pierce
Should be provoking pride that's fierce.
Applaud The Great Emancipator;
Educate an Adams-hater.
Grant Madison what he is due,
Be fair regarding Harding too
And share what Hoover means to you.
Wear cardigans for Carter's years
And give McKinley hearty cheers.
Spread Cleveland's fame without dissension;
Old Hickory deserves some mention.
Keep Woodrow Wilson jokes suppressed;
Chester A. Arthur did his best.
Imagine them all, if you will,
On Ronald Reagan's mythic hill.

II. Inside Jokes

Houseguests

There's shouting by the stove (it's Plath & Hughes)
as Wystan wanders off without his shoes
and Whitman picks the Cheetos off his beard.
The Ginsberg-Larkin chat is getting weird,
for after countless hours they have found
bizarre pornography is common ground.
Old Emily is not
As prim as billed —
When Dylan finds her bra-hooks —
She is thrilled.
Poe strokes his bird; Pound yawps that it's a pity
that T.S. can't sleep without his kitty.
Rimbaud's on eBay searching for a zebra
while sneering, "*Oui*, a *cheemp* can write *vers libre!*"
The Doctor's soggy chickens start to smell
and Wallace has insurance he must sell.
The readings are spectacular, I know,
but is there any way to make them go?

Letter to Auden

Uh, Wystan?
> Please forgive my arrogance;
> You know how most Americans impose.
Your chat with Byron gave me confidence
> That your Platonic ghost would not oppose
> Some verse disturbing you from your repose.
Besides, there's time to kill now that the Lord
Has silenced Merrill and his Ouija board.

Or do you pine for peace in Paradise,
> Besieged by every half-baked psychic hack
Intent on mining gems from your advice?
> With me, please don't insist on writing back
> Unless you can't resist some biting crack.
I also recognize that I had better
Keep my remarks far shorter than your *Letter*.

Indeed, I'll need substantial guile and nerve
> To try to emulate your bracing pace.
At twenty-nine, your lines had style and verve;
> My work at thirty-nine seems commonplace
> And foreordained to sink without a trace.
In any case, I do not hold out hope
Of sharing space with you or spiteful Pope.

A partial consolation on bad days
> Is no contemporary can compete
With you at all. Downtrodden MFAs

Denounce the Audenesque as obsolete
        Oppression by your dead-white-male-elite,
But then they go on to become depressed
Because there's nothing left to be confessed.

Only a few eccentrics still support
        Those poets who can scan lines properly.
However, I'm delighted to report
        That you became a hot pop property
        When *Four Weddings* exhumed your poetry.
You would have been amused to see its star
Arrested with a hooker in his car

But shocked that we remain so schizophrenic.
        Our sordid scandals rarely stay concealed
Although we want things guiltless and hygienic.
        Gay Studies has developed as a field
        In which great writers' lovers are revealed;
You lose some points for marrying a Mann
        And your diversity of goings-on.

As your long-suffering but faithful fan,
        I must disclose you missed the NEA,
The disco era, Gump and daily bran.
        In short, you would assess the present day
        As drearily debased and déclassé.
Well, Wystan, that is all that I can muster.
        Give my regards to Byron.

                        Fondly,
                        Juster

Honest Email to the Librarian of Congress

Attached please find my resume.
I see your website says today
you're searching for a Laureate.
For me it's not the glory it
bestows upon the honoree.
Lord knows, I'd take it on for free
because for me it is seductive
to "work" while being unproductive:
no weekly meetings to attend;
no more expenses to defend;
my repartee would not provoke
those HR chats about some joke.
Desk, paper, pen, humongous walls —
I will accept if Congress calls!
Although it's undeniable
I'm labeled "unreliable,"
I often show up right on time.
I write free verse, delight in rhyme,
and blandly fake my way through speeches
just like a Harvard guy who teaches.
The rehab stint has redefined me;
the hygiene issue is behind me.
Most people find my pit bull pleasant;
no books are overdue at present.

Rejection Note
for *Paradise Regained*

Loved that first book — it's got no equal —
but, Johnny, we don't love your sequel.
If you would only take a chance
on self-help or a gay romance,
we'd let you keep your last advance.
Phony conspiracies would do
if you could find a hook or two
for someone famous who won't sue.
Marketing knows you'll see the light,
and thinks Da Vinci is just right.

After 277 Years, Another Birthday Poem for Esther Johnson, a Long-term "Houseguest" of the Reverend Jonathan Swift

Let's overlook your death; it's time
To bless your birth with one more rhyme
And pray the Dean's unyielding spirit
Is lurking near enough to hear it.
I pay his debt with gratitude
Because I know that brackish mood
Which is the price of biting wit.
You made two opposites a fit
And smuggled joy into his life,
Although you never were a wife
And never worked a day for pay.
The scholars fuss with what to say
Because they do not see their blindness
In matters shaped by human kindness,
But, "Stella," on this day I praise
Your loyal and enduring ways —
And smirk when academics squirm.
With confidence I can affirm
That since you entered Heaven's walls,
No angel wrings its wings or calls
Your gentle interventions odd
When Swift is thundering at God.

Prufrock's Thirteen Ways of Looking at a Red Wheelbarrow Glazed with Rain beside White Chickens

Piove molto ogni mattina;
c'e aqua nella piscine.
Servono pollo di mare.
Chi ci viene a trovare?

I.

Let us go then, you and I,
As the stench spreads out around the sty
Like a drumstick decomposing on a table.
Let us go, through certain half-deserted coops,
Through mounds of chicken poop,
And farmhouse kitchens filled with roach motels
Just down the road from Haddam's Taco Bells.

II.

The red wheelbarrow left out in the rain
Lingers in a pool that will not drain.

III.

So much depends upon this easy tool
Though the help should use it, as a rule.

IV.

And indeed there will be time
To wonder, "Should I push" and "Should I push?"
Time to count the poultry in the bush.

V.

I grow old . . . I grow old.
My side dish is getting cold.

VI.

Dare I dine upon a nugget?
I shall wear white flannel trousers, like Colonel Sanders' pants.

VII.

But though I have wept and ordered, wept and paid,
Though I have seen my hens brought in on a platter,
I have seen the hot coils of the broiler flicker
And I have seen the short-order cook pick his nose and snicker,
And, in short, I felt fileted.

VIII.

There will be time, there will be time
To prepare the livers and the meat;
There will be time to slowly marinate,
And time for all the works and days of hands
That softly slop some gravy on your plate.

IX.

So much depends upon this deep-fried scene . . .
Oh do not ask just what I mean.

X.

Oh do not ask, "What is squawking?"
Let us go and keep on walking.

XI.

I should have been a pair of chicken feet
Dangling from a butcher's hook.

XII.

In the yard the chickens come and go
Flapping as the randy roosters crow.

XIII.

And I have heard them all, heard them all.
I have heard white chickens call.
I am not a farmer, nor was meant to be.
I do not think these chickens cluck for me.

Final Exam

Professor A.M. Juster

English 79b: Anagrammatic Perspectives
on 19ᵗʰ & 20ᵗʰ Century Poetry

Instructions: Rearrange letters of each word or phrase to form the name of a poet covered in this class.

Note: Self-grading on an honor system, including a two-hour time limit. A grade of 65 satisfies course requirements (40 for current Harvard students, 35 for alumni). Failing students are morally required to send their $10 tuition refund to: Measure Press, 526 South Lincoln Drive, Evansville, IN 47714. All refunds are final and unappealable.

A) (2 points each) TOILETS; DAZE OR PUN; HANDS GONE; SADLY A MONTH; HONK A JEST: A VAST PHILLY: A HOT DRY MASH; BALLING GREENS; O HUMAN SEA; COY PEW END; STONE ANNEX.

B) (4 points each) CATTLE WORKED; COILED WARS; TOUCH VIGOR; VALET CLAWS SEEN; SILKY DENIM ICON; LOW TROLL BEER.

C) (6 points each) DOPES FEN A SONAR; SOBERLY KNOWN GOD: HEARTY PORK ROD: MALTIER BEAUTY SWILL: RELAX PUKE IN HANDS; A CLOUDY TILLER AGES MORE; A MAIL WAR WILL SLIM COILS; HARD ON LOWER SAMPLE; PINK HAIR HILL.

EXTRA CREDIT: (8 points each) MONSTER MORTAR TATS; DEVIL CAMEL NINNY TATS.

III. The Stuttering Ventriloquist

Excerpts from
The Billy Collins Experience

Love Song

from Rapture with Paperclips *(2003)*

They say you have to love yourself
to love another
and so for you, dear,
only for you,
I am focusing on myself.

I wore my silk pajamas all day long
in case the moment was right.
Mid-morning, yellow roses arrived;
I was touched by my gesture,
but before long
they wilted in the kitchen window.
Later, there was chocolate —
rich, *erotic* chocolate —
but within minutes it made me feel fat.

A passionate note to myself
only ignored my issues,
and I never seem to talk
to myself anymore.
I have even become insensitive to my own needs.
Perhaps, my love, the answer
is couples therapy.

Self-portraits

from Gerald Ford Eaten by Wolves *(2005)*

I wake in ordinary light
and go downstairs
for toast and coffee.

The challenge of the day
is writing a poem
called "Self-portrait."

It is slow to come,
for it is tedious to find words
that are apt but not totally self-absorbed.

Yes, one can lower one's standards,
as it is said many poets do,
but I am not there yet.

Then it occurred to me on this day
a true self-portrait would portray
me writing a self-portrait,

which would spawn an infinite regress
of me's writing self-portraits
out to an infinite horizon.

I see myself as Whitmanesque multitudes,
like images in facing mirrors
or bacteria multiplying in Petri dishes.

I am content with the concept,
but forced to concede that other minds
might find it unsettling.

I run a hot bath and mull why z,
the fastest letter, comes at the end.
It is not easy for words to become literature.

Taxonomy

from Forgetting about Amnesia *(2007)*

Readers familiar with my *persona*
imagine someone gentle;
they would be knocked for a loop
to learn I categorize those around me
as animals, fish or insects.

I have neighbors,
a hippo and a flamingo —
no wonder they are childless.

There is an editor who is a jackal,
a poet who is a feral poodle,
and a beady-eyed *Post* reporter who is,
to be sure, a moray eel.

My attorney is a praying mantis,
or perhaps an atheist mantis,
who stands impossibly tall and thin.
She rubs her long fingers incessantly,
nibbles on my green cash.

Casually, she rips off the heads
of other helpless mantises
and gnaws on their skulls.
The lifeless faces of her victims
always have the same blank alien stare
as hers.

Crowded Skies

from Forgetting about Amnesia *(2007)*

As a matter of fact, I did notice
a sow followed by a string of piglets,
straining to stay airborne
with their unfamiliar wings
as they crossed my line of vision
outside the kitchen window.

Then the doorbell rang,
and I found a crisply dressed
but sumptuous woman at my door.
She announced she was
from the Registry of Motor Vehicles,
apologized for the long lines of the past,
and handed me my new license.
When she asked if there was anything else
she could do for me,
I had a failure of imagination.

Then the phone throbbed.
It was Blue Cross Blue Shield,
apologizing for the three years
they spent trying to bill me
for a very expensive hysterectomy
I never had.
They said they fired the incompetents,
simplified everything,
and my next operation was on them.

When the mail came that afternoon,
there was a sweet-smelling, handwritten note
from the cheerleader who rejected
my invitation to the junior prom.
She regretted any distress
her handling of that matter
might have caused me.

I gather air traffic controllers
are up in arms about the crowded skies,
but they will work it out,
I'm sure.

On the Road

from Avocados in Action *(2008)*

Dylan Thomas once said at a reading,
"There are no poetry audiences,
just occasional gatherings of eccentrics."

I am concerned, even intermittently panicked,
that my agent, Francine, accepted this wisdom
with way too much enthusiasm.

Yesterday I headlined a convention
of Klingon speakers; I would read a poem,
then listen to the translation before reading another.

I suppose my nose *was* out of joint —
though I am not convinced that noses *have* joints.
My translator's applause was longer and louder.

Today it was an enormous group
of Vietnam War reenactors
who shouted me down with protest slogans.

Tomorrow it is a college conference on poetry
and S&M. By phone I asked the organizer
which poems he wanted me to read.

He reassured me in soothing tones:
"Any of them will satisfy half the group,
and the others can't wait for Q & A."

Book 1, Satire 9

As I was strolling down the Sacred Way
for no real reason, pondering some stray
idea with the utmost concentration,
this fellow whom I know by reputation
comes running up and grabs my hand.

                              "So how
are you, dear friend?"

                   "Quite well, until just now,"
was my reply.

         "I wish you all the best!"

As he continues being quite a pest,
I snap,

      "What *is* it *now*?"

                    and he's complaining,
"You must know me — I've had first-class training!"

so I say,

      "I'm *horribly* impressed!"

To shake this boor who's making me distressed,
I walk more quickly, then abruptly veer
away and whisper in my servant's ear
as streams of sweat cascade onto my feet.
I murmur, "Oh Bolanus, what a treat
to have your temper!" as the boor heaps praise
on every precinct in so many ways
he praises Rome in its entirety.

When I do not respond, he lectures me,
"You're in an awful hurry to break loose.
I've noticed that in you — but it's no use.
I'll stand beside you all along the way!"

"There *really* is no need for you to stay.
I need to visit someone you don't know;
he's sick in bed, and I will *have* to go
across the Tiber near the parks of Caesar."

"I'm not engaged in anything but leisure,
and I'm not sluggish; I will follow you."

I drop my ears as sullen donkeys do
when overloaded. He begins to sell
with, "If I have done my self-assessment well,
when choosing friends, you should evaluate
me as a person you'd appreciate
far more than Varius and Viscus, for
who cranks out verse as quickly? Or much more?
Who moves with greater grace? Hermogenes
himself would envy my sweet melodies!"

I have to break in.
                    "Do you have a mother
who must be supported? Or another
relative?"
                    "Nobody. I have laid
them all to rest."

                    What luck for them! I've stayed
behind, so finish me off as I near

a fate predicted by a Sabine seer
who, in my boyhood, saw my destiny
by shaking urns, and sang these lines to me:

No poison herb or hostile herb will slay him;
nor TB, whooping cough or gout dismay him.
A blabbermouth will suck the air around him;
he must avoid a gasbag who will hound him.

Having consumed a quarter of the day
already, both of us then make our way
to Vesta's temple, where by accident
he learns he'll forfeit to a litigant
if he does not officially appear
in court for his defense. "Assist me here
a little if you are my friend!" he pleads.

"Damn me if I possess what someone needs
to testify or understand our laws!
I have to hurry off, you know the cause."

He says, "I wonder what I ought to do —
should I abandon my response or you?"

"Me please!"

        "I shall not do it!" he replies.
Because it's risky to antagonize
a person who you know you just can't whip,

I follow him.
        "Is your relationship

good with Maecenas?"
                              He begins again,
". . . a man who has few friends, but acumen.
Nobody's wiser when he makes a bet.
If you would introduce me, you would get
an ardent advocate, a number two.
Damn me if there's someone we won't outdo!"

"The way we're living there is different
from what you think; our group's more innocent
and free of vices. I'm not agitated
if someone's richer or more educated.
Each to his own."
                         "That's quite a tale you weave,
although it is not easy to believe."

"Yet, nonetheless, it is the truth."
                                    "You fire
me up with even more intense desire
to be his confidant!"
                         "You can express
your interest; with all your manliness
I'm sure you can prevail. You can rely
on him to drop his guard, which tells you why
it's hard to get a meeting with the man."

"I will not be deflected from my plan!
I'll bribe his slaves! If first I fail, I'll fight
and never stop! I'll find the time that's right!
I'll chase him through the public squares! I'll go
accompany him! 'Life does not bestow
its benefits on man without hard work.'"

As he continues acting like a jerk,
Aristius Fuscus, my cherished friend,
who knows him full well, comes around the bend.
We take a break. He asks, "Where have you been?"
and "Any plans?" then chatters. I begin
to tug upon his toga and to prod
his unresponsive arm, then wink and nod
for rescue. Joking with an evil twist,
he smirks and keeps pretending he has missed
what's going on. I'm getting steaming mad.

"I'm *positive* you told me that we had
a matter for *discreet* consideration."

"I do recall. We'll have that conversation
at a better moment. With today
the thirtieth — the Sabbath — would you say
something offensive to the dock-tailed Jew?"

I say, "I hold no superstitious views."

"Not so for me. I am a bit more weak,
part of the crowd. Forgive me, we will speak
some other time."

        To think so bleak a sun
is hanging over me! The shameless one
escapes and leaves me on the edge. By chance,
he meets his plaintiff face-to-face, who rants,
"Where are you going now, you piece of scum?"
Then turns to me to ask, "Will you become
my witness?" Then I let him touch my ear;

they're off to court. Loud shouts are all I hear,
and crowds race everywhere without direction
(Apollo's way of giving me protection).

(Translated from the Latin of Horace)

Book 2, Satire 5

Ulysses: "Tiresias, I want more information!
                This question needs a fuller explanation:
                What kind of merchandise and strategy
                would make me whole again financially?
                …Why do you laugh?"

Tiresias: "For you, most shrewd of men,
                why isn't it enough to sail again
                to Ithaca, and then to cast your eyes
                upon your house?"

Ulysses: "O you who tell no lies,
                why can't you see? I've come back home stripped clean
                of cash and assets, as you had foreseen,
                and hordes of opportunists did not spare
                the herds and storage cellars I had there.
                What's more, without some cash a noble birth
                and virtue do not match what seaweed's worth!"

Tiresias: "To be blunt, since it's poverty you dread,
                discover new techniques to get ahead!
                Suppose you have a thrush or some such thing;
                you should release it, letting it take wing
                until it finds a glittering estate
                that's owned by someone old. The Lar can wait
                so he can taste; send fruit and products raised
                upon your tidy farm and have him praised
                above the Lar. Though he has always lied,

lacked breeding, stained his hands with fratricide,
and slipped his chains, when walking you should go
along the outside if he wants it so."

Ulysses: "What! Cover up some dirty Dama's flank?
              At Troy, against the men of highest rank,
              that's not how I behaved."

Tiresias: "Then you'll be poor."

Ulysses: "I'll make my steadfast soul endure this chore;
              I've done worse.
                                Fortune teller that you are,
              enlighten me right now about how far
              I need to go to rake in cash and wealth."

Tiresias: "I've *told* you, and I tell you now: use stealth
              while trawling for the wills of older men
              in every place that you can find, and then
              if one or more have nibbled on the bait
              but slipped away, don't brood or hesitate
              to hone your craft despite your consternation.
              Wherever there is Forum litigation
              (whether minor or significant)
              become a lawyer for the litigant
              who's rich and childless, though a jerk — the sort
              who hauls a better person into court
              without a bit of shame or legal basis.
              Shun the citizen with stronger cases
              or a pedigree if there's a son
              or fertile wife at home. Tell anyone
              called 'Publius' or "Quintus' (first names please

their precious ears):
                              Your moral qualities
have made us allies. I have learned that laws
are two-edged swords: I can defend a cause
of action. I would rather let my eyes
be plucked you than for you to realize
a loss on trinkets or be vilified.

Send him back home to tend his tender hide,
and then you will become his advocate!
Persist relentlessly and never quit
regardless 'if the scarlet Dogstar splits
the silent statues' or, if stuffed with bits
of rich tripe, Furius 'is spewing drops
of spit on snowy Alpine mountaintops.'
Someone will nudge another, then complain,
'Why can't you see how he has suffered pain,
provided help to friends, and been astute?'

More tuna will be swimming down this route,
and ponds will bulge. What's more if someone wealthy
has a son, acknowledged but unhealthy,
you should, in order not to be betrayed
by obvious attention you have paid
to someone single, cozy up with care
and hope that you are named the backup heir,
then if some tragic fluke should take the son
to Orcus, it will leave you as the one
to fill the void.

                              These gambits should succeed.

If given his last testament to read,
be sure that you refuse and push away
the tablets as you subtly survey
arrangements covered in the second line
of Page One. Quickly see if there's some sign
that you're sole heir or with a multitude.
Often the minor bureaucrat re-brewed
to be a magistrate deceives the crow
whose beak has split as far as it can go,
and Nascia, who hunts a legacy,
will give Coranus grounds for levity."

Ulysses: "Are you insane? Or is it that you tease
                me by revealing doubtful prophecies?"

Tiresias: "O scion of Laertes, all these things
                that I describe are what the future brings,
                or not, for great Apollo gives to me
                the gift of seeing what will come to be."

Ulysses: "But, nonetheless, provide me, if you're able,
                with interpretation of your fable."

Tiresias: "The moment will arrive when a young man,
                despised by Parthians, born of the clan
                of eminent Aeneas, will command
                respect from everyone on sea and land,
                while Nasica's tall daughter (she who dreads
                to *satisfy* her obligations), weds
                the brave Coranus. After this event,
                the son-in-law has something to present:
                he tries to give the father of his bride

his will and have it read, though he's denied
a while by Nasica, who in the end
reads silently and comes to comprehend
that neither he nor relatives received
bequests — except a reason to be peeved!

I'll add this point to that: if some old guy
who's lost his mind can be 'persuaded' by
a shrew and freedman, treat them as your team!
Praise them so they will speak of their esteem
for you when you're away.
                                        This helps as well:
it's best that *you* assault the citadel.
Suppose this idiot is writing verse
that couldn't possibly be any worse,
I'd praise it! Does he like his one-night stands?
Beware if he must tell you his demands!
Make sure the better person in the deal
will get Penelope."

Ulysses: "*What?* You don't feel,
do you, she's someone you could procure,
she who has been so virtuous and pure,
whom all those suitors never led astray?"

Tiresias: "I do! The youngsters who would come her way
were chintzy, zealous for her recipes,
not Venus — which explains Penelope's
devotion. But if she tastes just a bit
of geezer-generated benefit
from entering a partnership with you,
just like some bitch with greasy hides to chew,

she won't be scared away. Let me unfold
a tale that happened back when I was old:
an ancient nasty hag at Thebes was hauled
away for burial like this: as called
for in her will, a semi-naked heir conveyed
her well-oiled body so she could evade
his clutches through the last resort of dying.
I think her motive was he kept on trying
to be grabby while she was alive.

Tread carefully. Don't shirk or overstrive.
A bigmouth ticks off those who snarl and frown;
say only 'yes' and 'no.' Keep ducking down
like Davus in the comedy; appear
as if you've totally succumbed to fear.
Approach obsequiously. If winds rise,
some covering is what you should advise
for his beloved head. What you must do
in crowded areas is plow right through
with shoulders low so he escapes the throng.
Lend him an ear though he has talked too long.
Does he delight in being overpraised?
Until he says, "*Enough!*" with both hands raised
up to the heavens, you should press the matter
and inflate the windbag with your chatter.

When he has freed you from long servitude,
and worry, and you know with certitude
it's not a dream, you'll hear, 'A quarter-share
is given to Ulysses as the heir!'
Say, 'Now my buddy Dama has departed!
Who could be as loyal and stout-hearted?'

If you're somewhat able, shed a tear
to hide your joy. Don't make the tomb austere
if you select it; let your neighbors praise
the classiness the funeral displays.
If there's an older co-heir who keeps hacking,
assure him if a farm or house is lacking
in his share, you would be serious
about deep discounts.
                              Now imperious
Proserpine is dragging me of to Hell!
Have a good life, and I must say farewell!"

(Translated from the Latin of Horace)

Poem of the Prick

By God, you prick, now I will have to try
To guard you with my hand and wary eye.
Named in her claims, you stiffened, head-high stick,
I'll stare far harder at your every trick.
You're prey for pussy traps; since her complaint
Your snout must wear a bridle for constraint;
To fend off re-indictment, show more care
So minstrels do not warble their despair!
My view of you, my wicked wooden rod,
My scrotum's horn, is: do not rise or prod!
You gift to every noble Christian miss,
You earth-nut cudgel of the lap's abyss,
Just like a strangled gander in a heap
With all its yearling plumage, you should sleep!
With your wet head, your neck with milky spray,
Your sprout tipped, keep hot gripping hands away!
O blighted, blunted one, infernal pole,
Prime pillar for a girl's bisected whole,
A hollowed conger eel whose head's not limber,
Blunt barrier, like hazel trees' fresh timber,
In size far larger than a big lug's thighs,
For evening prowls the wedge that satisfies,
An auger like a post that's carved from wood —
The one called "tail" who wears a leather hood —
You are the lover's lever for a pass,
The bolt for shutters on a girl's bare ass.
You have a pipe inside your head to play
That whistle cuing you to screw each day.

There is an eye high on your brow that sees
Each woman's most attractive qualities.
A rounded pestle, ordnance as it aims,
Stokes tiny pussies' Purgatory flames.
You are the thatching-rake for girlish laps,
The bell-tongue's sudden music as it claps,
A dumb husk digging by the fairy walls,
A pouch of skin, a nose that grows two balls.
You are a pant-load pumping up for sex.
Your neck is leathery like ganders' necks,
You total fraud, seed-pod of fornication,
Hard nail that causes pain and litigation!
Recall the writ and the indictment now.
Head, plow for planting children, you should bow.
Restraining you is hard work to sustain;
Indeed, pathetic poker, you're a pain!
Swipes at your master often are severe;
The filthiness inside your head is clear.

(Translated from the Middle Welsh of Dafydd ap Gwilym)

Poem of the Pussy

Our poets are on each and every day,
Just sodden clods, their dullness on display.
I do not guarantee praise he may spread
Since this long line of mine is so well-bred.
For girls around the world he's always made
A show of love-songs, though they're badly played.
A gift as partial penance is a bother
Until he seals the deal, by God the Father.
He praises dress and tresses for their "flair"
And every living lass will pass as "fair."
He gladly praises eyebrows and what's high;
No region down below them is passed by.
He also praises fleshiness possessed
By any supple, smooth and buxom breast,
And throws out glowing terms for hands and arms
As well as any of her higher charms.
As evening falls, his magical summation
Is taking place in song and conversation.
God, with His gift of grace, has suffered through
The barren blather of this overview.
Bereft of praise, her middle part is spurned
Together with the spot where heirs are earned.
A cozy pussy has clear confidence
As a plump, soft, sore ring of excellence.
You are a wholesome and appealing place,
You, lovers' pussy, with your charm and lace,
A body part whose vigor is profound,
That fringe and fat around a somber mound.

Behold in disbelief the region where
A ring's equipped with lips and pubic hair!
Your valley's deeper than a hand or ladle,
A ditch in which a two-hand prick can cradle.
Cunt, near the swollen rear is your domain,
A split red platform for his sweet refrain,
And, for more ample tops, the Church's men
(those glowing saints!) are never timid when
They have good odds to get a special deal;
By Beuno, they will cop a splendid feel!
For this technique, relentlessly critique
Those know-it-alls within the poets' clique.
If we let pussy poems proliferate,
Their value surely will appreciate.
Like silk in sultans' odes, the veil in front
Of the slight seam (the spritely, beaming cunt)
Waves in tight space in place of a "Hello!"
You, bush, are sour; you are love-soaked, though.
Fine, feisty forest, thoughtful gift for her,
Twin balls within your cozy scarf of fur,
A girl's dense thatch, a trysting place one day,
Becoming bush, may God protect your way!

(Translated from the Middle Welsh of Gwerful Mechain)

Epitaph for a Drunken Twit

Peace, traveler. Read with the lines unheard —
just as priests mumble through The Holy Word —
so noise won't take away sweet sleep and make
my gullet dry whenever I awake,
for I, a snoring twit stone hides from sight,
was once great Bacchus' famed acolyte
because I spent four decades on a bender.
Next, slumber slyly made my eyes surrender,
as when one's limbs are soaked with lots of wine,
and, having spent my prime in sweet decline,
my life and boozing reached their ends in sync
(though one might think that I still dream or drink
since, as I doze, I chatter anyhow).
Traveler, good-bye. Go in silence now.

(Translated from the Latin of Erasmus)

Martialed Arguments

1.1

Here's what you read, what you demand:
Martial! Renowned throughout the land!
Small books that turn a witty phrase!
Close reader, glory that you gave
a living, feeling man is praise
few poets get before the grave.

1.4

Caesar, if you peruse my books,
please soften your majestic looks.
Great leaders are the butts of jokes,
but they ignore our friendly pokes.
So read my poetry, I pray,
the way you would a comic play —
and give your goons some latitude.
My lines are lewd, but *I'm* a prude.

1.9

Dear Cotta:

You think you're pretty great
and so you pose and primp,
but such a man I rate
a pretty, grating wimp.

1.16

Some poems are proficient;
some poems are sufficient.
More poems are rubbish
that you are reading here,
Avitus, but it's clear
that is one way to publish.

1.20

Tell me, Cecil, what madness is among us?
Your consumption of mushrooms has stung us!
What prayers could spare a gut so humongous?
Here's hoping you gorge on poisonous fungus!

1.23

Nobody, Cotta, has been able
to get a seating at your table
unless he met you in a bath.
I wondered how I earned your wrath
but then deduced I had some flaw
when you last saw me in the raw.

1.28

To say Acerra stinks of day-old booze is wrong!
Each drink is freshened all night long!

1.47

Diaulus was a physician;
now he's a mortician.
The undertaking's the same —
it just has a new name.

1.57

Dear Flaccus:

What sort of girl do I enjoy?
One not too slutty or too coy —
between the two I'm satisfied.
I won't be glutted or denied.

1.73

Your unpossessive attitude
ensured your wife would not be screwed —
but now that you have posted sentries,
legions are pursuing entries.
Maecilianus, you are shrewd.

1.83

Dear Manneia:

Your lapdog's licking your lips and chin;
no wonder with that shit-eating grin.

1.89

Dear Cinna:

You always chat in every ear
though no one's there to overhear.
You cry and sigh, laugh and accuse;
you shout and pout, sing and effuse.
Your sickness is so deeply rooted
that even Caesar's praise is muted.

1.91

Dear Laelius:

You won't reveal your verse,
but whine that mine is worse.
Just leave me alone
or publish your own.

2.4

O Ammianus,
how tender is your mother!
And, Ammianus,
you clearly can't resist her!
She's always cooing "brother"
and you respond with "sister."
Why are these naughty names
essential to your games?
What's wrong with reality?
You call this frivolity?
It isn't real. A mother who aspires
to seem a sister hides her true desires.

2.8

Your judge and your lawyer want theirs from the trough.
Sextus, I advise you to just pay them off.

2.20

Paul is reciting poems he buys.
At least he doesn't plagiarize.

2.25

Dear Galla:

I only get delay,
not what I desire;
Refuse me right away
if you're still a liar.

2.42

Dear Zoilus:

Your ass in the sink
is making it stink.
For a fouler smell,
dear Zoilus,
dunk your head as well.

2.52

Dasius handles his accounts;
buxom Spatale's bathing fee
required gold for three.
She paid him those amounts.

3.9

They say that Cinna slams
me in his epigrams.
A poem no one has heard
has really not occurred.

3.18

Dear Max:

Your reading opened with a whine
about your laryngitis,
but since your alibi was fine
why read on and incite us?

3.54

You're far too rich for me,
Galla, with your price so high.
A simple "no" would be
a more straightforward reply.

3.70

Dear Scaevinus,

Aufinia, your ex-wife,
is spicing up your sex life;
your former competition
is assuming your position.
As your wife, she was unexciting,
so why is she now so inviting?

3.79

Sex with Sertorius is anticlimactic;
rapid withdrawal is his typical tactic.

3.94

You gripe the rabbit's rare
and so you grip the whip.
Rufus! You carve the cook
and yet you spare the hare.

4.12

Dear Thais:

There's nobody who you won't screw,
but if that can't embarrass you,
feel shame at least for what is true:
Thais, there's nothing you won't do.

4.24

Every friend of Lycoris has lost her life.
Fabianus, he should meet my wife.

4.38

Galla, refuse me!
Without a wait
or some hard trial,
love won't amuse me.
So hesitate
(just for a while . . .).

4.48

Papylus, you delight in being sodomized,
then weep and come off traumatized.
Do you regret, Papylus, what you've done
or are you mourning your lost fun?

4.69

Papylus, you may try
the Setine or the Massic,
but rumors keep us dry —
though your wines *are* classic.
It's being said of you
four dead wives shared that glass.
I don't believe it's true,
Papylus, but I'll pass.

5.81

Dear Aemilianus:

If you are poor, you'll stay that way.
Only the rich get rich today.

6.2

Adultery and child castration
were laughed off as a game,
but, Caesar, since your legislation,
we do not stray or maim.
You spared the coming generation
from our longstanding shame,
since whores and eunuchs in our nation
were frequently the same.

6.7

This month "the family values bill"
makes adultery a crime.
With nine divorces, Telesilla still
wants a wedding one more time.
Instead of phony weddings by the score,
I would choose an honest whore.

6.22

Dear Proculina:

You marry your lover
to hide indiscretion.
Whatever the cover,
it's still a confession.

6.48

Dear Pomponius:

A crowd in togas shouts its gratitude.
It's not for you; it's for your food!

6.63

Dear Marianus:

You know why he is fishing
and what he wants to net.
You know what he is wishing
and what he wants to get,
but still he's in your will,
you foolish imbecile.

"He gave my pricey gifts," you note,
but that was just the lure.
What breed of fish would ever dote
on fishermen? How sure
are you his grieving will be honest?
If you want true sorrow
postmortem, Marianus,
then cut him off tomorrow.

6.87

Dear Caesar:

I pray you may receive your due
from all the gods (including you).
If worthy, grant my wishes too.

7.3

Dear Pontilianus:

You wonder why my little book is overdue,
dear Pontilianus?
It's just that I don't want to look at one from you.

7.4

Dear Castricus:

Oppianus was so pallid
he began to write a ballad.

7.16

In light of my troubles,
I've cleaned out my coffers.
I'm hocking your baubles —
care to make me an offer?

7.24

Carisianus has an abnormal air;
he goes to Saturnalia in formal wear.

7.58

Dear Galla:

Since you adore long hair
and whiskers trimmed with care,
you've had your wedding days
with six or seven gays.
Though you may test their strength
and limping pricks at length,
they nonetheless withstand
your tired hand's demand.
You leave the dolled-up room,
then dump your mincing groom,
only to reappear
with others just as queer.
You should be looking for
tough types who talk of war —
some husky hairy guy;
you'll find him if you try,
although the straightest scenes
do have their share of queens.
Galla, what an ordeal
to wed a man who's real!

7.65

Dear Gargilianus:

You wearied as you snowed three courts
through twenty winters of litigation.
Poor fool! What sort of man resorts
to choosing decades of frustration?

7.77

Dear Tucca:

You nag me for my little books,
but I refuse what you demand.
You wouldn't give them second looks
and would just dump them second-hand.

7.91

Smooth-talking Juvenal, look! From my own field
I send you Saturnalian nuts.
The scarecrow's other produce from this yield
was given by a lusty prick to sluts.

8.35

Since you both share the same approach to life
(a lousy husband and a lousy wife),
I am bewildered it
is not a better fit.

8.43

Chrestilla buries husbands;
Fabius buries wives.
Venus, please pair these winners
so that neither one survives.

8.53

Oh fairest of the fair,
yet cruel beyond compare,
Catulla, why aren't you
less gorgeous or more true?

8.69

Dear Vacerra:

You pine for bards of old
and poets safely cold.
Excuse me for ignoring your advice,
but good reviews from you aren't worth the price.

9.4

Galla will screw
if you pay two,
and do far more
if you pay four.
So, Aeschylus,
something's amiss
for *ten*! For what?
Her mouth is shut.

9.9

Dear Cantharus:

Although you enjoy the free fare,
you drone on and bully and swear.
I suggest you try to be more discreet;
you must eat your words, if you want to eat.

9.10

Paula wants to marry Priscus
because he is so clever.
Wise choice. As for his wishes,
he's wisely saying, "Never!"

9.33

When the bathhouse breaks into loud applause,
you will know that well-hung Maro is the cause.

9.78

Dear Picentius:

With seven husbands now expired,
Galla married you.
I think that Galla has desired
you be buried too.

9.81

Dear Aulus:

The public likes my little books
although some poet calls them "crude."
Who cares? When I'm preparing food
I'd rather please my guests than cooks.

10.9

I, Martial, am known in every nation
for hendecasyllabic versification
and abundant, though well-tempered, wit.
So why do you feel inadequate?
I am still not famous, of course,
compared to Andraemon the horse.

10.43

Your seventh wife, Phil, is buried in your field.
Nobody gets from land, Phil, that kind of yield.

10.47

These things, my Martialis,
can always give me solace:
wealth that's unmerited
since it's inherited;
land yielding fair returns;
a fire that always burns;
a lack of legal woes
or need for formal clothes;
peace and tranquility;
manly nobility;
good health, an earnest way
without naïveté;
close friends, a party scene;
straight-forward, good cuisine;

a night's sobriety
without anxiety;
a marriage bed that's plain
and yet not too mundane;
dark hours one can keep
far shorter with some sleep;
accept life; don't aspire
to being something higher.
Don't fear, or ever pray,
to see that final day.

10.57

I used to eagerly await
your pound of silver plate,
but now it's pepper in amounts
you measure by the ounce.
Sextus, I have no need of spice
that comes at that high price.

11.35

Dear Fabullus:

You invite some mob
who I don't know,
then bitch and sob
when I don't show.
I'm just not prone
to dine alone.

11.67

Dear Maro:

You stiff me, saying I
will get it when you die.
Unless you are a dope,
you know that's what I hope.

11.87

Dear Charidemus:

Once you were rich and gay,
and girls were kept at bay;
now you're reduced to rags
and chasing after hags.
How sad is desperation!
It forced your fornication.

11.97

Dear Telesilla:

Four times in one night is what I can do.
Damn! Once in four years is plenty with you.

11.103

Dear Safronius:

Your style and manner seem so mild
that I have doubts about your child.

12.9

Africanus has his millions, but is greedy.
Fortune pampers those who think they're needy.

12.30

Aper is sober and spare,
but I really do not care.
These qualities I commend
in a slave, but not a friend.

12.56

You monthly illness, Polycharmus,
doesn't hurt you, but does harm us.
After each recovery you're miffed
that you don't receive a get-well gift.
Polycharmus, your venality
calls for medical finality.

12.58

Your wife declares you crave
her girlish slave,
while she herself enjoys
your litter boys.
Alauda, this seems fair;
you're quite a pair.

12.61

Dear Ligurra:

You have become unhappy
not getting something snappy
from me, but you just want
to seem fair game to taunt.
Your phony fears and wishes
are overly ambitious;
Libyan lions roar
at bulls, but they ignore
the butterflies. Your aim
of literary fame
demands some drunken hack
from off the beaten track —
someone who would not balk
at scratching out in chalk
or coal the kind of pap
you flip through as you crap,
so do not have concern
your face might feel a burn

because I cannot stand
diminishing my brand.

12.69

Your good friends, Paul, are as genuine
as your chintzy prints and porcelain.

12.80

Callistratus praises everyone
no matter what they've done.
When no person ever comes up short,
what good is his report?

(Translated from the Latin of Martial)

To a Statue of Rufus the Rhetorician

Behold the new memorial
for one so professorial!
It's such a lifelike duplicate —
right down to lack of tongue or brains.
Stiff, dumb and blind — a perfect fit
(except no wimpiness remains).

(Translated from the Latin of Ausonius)

Myron Begged Lisa for Sex

Gray-haired Myron begged Lisa for sex,
but his pleas were promptly denied.
Since her thinking was hardly complex,
his white locks were hastily dyed.
With new hair but the same tired face,
he returned to reargue his case,
but upon her new suitor's arrival,
she was struck that he looked like the rival,
then said, "Idiot don't even bother —
I have already kissed off your father."

(Translated from the Latin of Ausonius)

Philomusus the Grammarian

Phil, do books bought at great expense
make you an academician?
Next you will buy some instruments
and claim that you are a musician.

(Translated from the Latin of Ausonius)

On the Man Who Found Treasure When He Meant to Hang Himself

A man who had knotted a noose
saw gold and cut himself loose.
The owner discovered the knot
and hoisted himself on the spot.

(Translated from the Latin of Ausonius)

On the Shyster Who Called His Whore "Grace"

If his words could equal his penis,
He'd be known as a legal genius.
He is up half the night
Missing laws he should cite
While joined by his servant of Venus.

(Translated from the Latin of Luxorius)

IV. Shrapnel

A Stern Warning to Canada

If you want peace,
withdraw your geese.

Advice for My Comrades

"Farewell" is hard until you try it,
      as when we gave up on gluten.
You could be free of Pussy Riot
      if you just gave up on Putin.

Gift Shop Blues

Bright postcards on a rack
acknowledge what we lack.
The most we can express
about our great vacation
takes a few lines or less,
and needs some illustration.

Juice

Mulberries fall; tart purple rots to wine.
Plump sparrows celebrate and gorge like swine.
Perhaps their revelry should be delayed
Since cats appreciate a marinade.

Mismatch

I kept hoping she would come alone.
She's a gem, but he's a kidney stone.

A Consolation of Aging

Despite my thinning hair,
no barber cuts his rate.
At least the airlines care
and do not charge by weight.

Disclaimer

Despite what's promised when you marry,
actual results may vary.

Revisionism

If you believe our liturgies,
        no marriage may be sundered,
but lawyers say six-figure fees
        can fix what God has blundered.

From the Workplace

Your Midlife Crisis

You found yourself, but at an awful cost.
We liked you better when you were lost.

To My Ambitious Colleague

Your uphill climb will never stop;
scum always rises to the top.

Concession to My Colleague

I know that you will win in time;
the rising sewage lifts all slime.

Selected Problems
in Interspecies Relationships
As Exemplified in Classical
Mythology

I.

Medusa dolled up for a date,
then hissed when he showed up late.
With true venom she said,
"I should cut off your head,
but now you're so stoned I must wait!"

II.

Pan wrote an amorous note
to a lass who was crass and remote,
but when someone horned in,
he piped up with a grin,
"You can't let a girl get your goat!"

III.

The Argonauts wanted a fling,
but Circe was running a sting.
When they oinked for relief,
she said, "I don't see your beef,
You wives won't notice a thing."

Greeting Card Verse
for Offbeat Occasions

Prostitution Arrest

I know the press recorded
Your alleged solicitation,
And though it seems quite sordid,
I just know you'll get probation.

Food Poisoning of Guest

I'm sorry my sashimi
Was rotting on the docks.
Whenever you next see me,
I'll only serve you lox.

Botched Intimate Tattoo

Your tattoo artist was a jerk
And sloppy in his spelling,
But given where he put his work,
Nobody will be telling.

Botches

These half-finished poems of mine
    lie in pieces on the floor
as if Doctor Frankenstein
    couldn't focus on his chore.

For Jim Henson

Only he could glam-
orize
a puppet with ham
for thighs

then make her libidin-
ous
for a frog's forbidden
kiss.

Elegy for a Horseshoe Crab

Here on the sand lies crusty *limulus*,
the stalwart crab of the marine Old Right.
Untouched by any trendy stimulus,
our kind assesses change in clear, cold light
before once more deciding to hold tight.

You chose not to evolve or to rebel.
Resisting odd mutations served you well.
Last rites like these should have solemnity;
I'm sorry children frolic with your shell.
Let's hope they are more somber when it's me.

Self-portrait at Fifty

None of this can be denied:
crabby, flabby, full of pride;
hypertensive, pensive, snide;
slowing, growing terrified.

Epitaph for a Star of Reality Shows

Despite his mansion and the maid,
He found more money to be made.
Near death he sold the broadcast rights
For his last words and his last rites.

On the Death of B.F. Skinner

The headlines were unanimous
from *Newsweek* to *Le Monde*;
no matter what the stimulus,
B.F did not respond.

Candid Headstone

Here lies what's left of Michael Juster,
A failure filled with bile and bluster.
Regard the scuttlebutt as true.
Dance on the grave; most others do.

The Author

A.M. Juster has worked in senior positions, including Commissioner of Social Security, for four Presidents of the United States, and has run three publicly traded biotechnology companies. The Alzheimer's Association has named him their Humanitarian of the Year, and he has received other major awards for his public service.

He is the author of four books of poetry translated from Latin and Italian, and he has won the Willis Barnstone Translation Prize for a translation from Middle Welsh. A three-time winner of the Howard Nemerov Sonnet Award, his book of original poetry won the Richard Wilbur Award. His work has appeared in *The Paris Review, Hudson Review, Poetry, Hopkins Review, Measure, Southwest Review, The New Criterion, Rattle, Arion, Light* and many other journals.

He is a graduate of Yale and Harvard with two honorary degrees.

CPSIA information can be obtained
at www.ICGtesting.com
Printed in the USA
LVOW12*2257271216
518912LV00017B/333/P